# The Loneliest Age

# The Loneliest Age

Poems by

Richard LeDue

© 2020 Richard LeDue. All rights reserved.
This material may not be reproduced in any form, published,
reprinted, recorded, performed, broadcast,
rewritten or redistributed without
the explicit permission of Richard LeDue.
All such actions are strictly prohibited by law.

Cover design by Shay Culligan
Cover photograph by Etienne Girardet at Unsplash

ISBN: 978-1-952326-59-2

Kelsay Books
502 South 1040 East, A-119
American Fork, Utah, 84003

# Acknowledgments

*Rue Scribe:* "Brothers and Sisters"

*The Mark Literary Review:* "The Loneliest Age"

*Crepe and Penn Literary Magazine:* "My Dead Neighbors," "Third Date"

*Eunoia Review:* "Sounds of Loneliness," "The North is No Place For Love"

*Adelaide Literary Magazine:* "Because The Doctor Recommended Walking," "In Bed With a Fever," "Loneliness is Rarely Imagined"

*Mojave He[art] Review:* "It Doesn't Take Much To Break Us," "We Were Always a Mirage"

*Tower Poetry Society:* "Dining Alone"

*Lite Lit One:* "Another Day"

*Little Rose Magazine:* "Wrong"

# Contents

| | |
|---|---|
| Brothers and Sisters | 11 |
| The Loneliest Age | 12 |
| My Dead Neighbors | 14 |
| Sounds of Loneliness | 15 |
| overdue goodbye | 16 |
| What Winter Sounds Like Now | 17 |
| Last Season | 18 |
| Because the Doctor Recommended Walking | 19 |
| In Bed with a Fever | 20 |
| Another Day | 21 |
| Growth | 22 |
| It Doesn't Take Much to Break Us | 23 |
| Third Date | 24 |
| We Were always a Mirage | 25 |
| lamentation | 26 |
| Dining Alone | 27 |
| Together | 28 |
| Needs | 29 |
| The Night Is Never Long Enough | 30 |
| The North Is No Place for Love | 31 |
| September Snow | 32 |
| Loneliness Is Rarely Imagined | 33 |
| Wrong | 34 |

# Brothers and Sisters

Abandoned among tall grass,
he panics,
runs so hard that the tomato soup
from lunch jumps up his throat,
burns away his fear,
leaves only anger,
while his older sister laughs-
all part of an ancient game
that no one bothered to give a name.

# The Loneliest Age

We didn't starve,
but were malnourished;
learned to read
from the back of cereal boxes
(part of a complete breakfast).

Our favorite TV shows
taught us
the joy of tearing plastic,
cardboard apart;
bedroom floor littered
with action figures like a battlefield
where everyone lost.

Adolescence was no better.
Toy soldiers buried
in shoe-boxes, no monument,
just acne and the realization
that childhood had too many bowls
filled with sugar.

Legally an adult at eighteen,
yet unkissed,
lips over licked,
especially in winter,
builds to a fantasy that sex
would mean someone
else to pour the milk.

Not elderly yet,
but envision a beautiful nurse,
sponge baths daily,
along with diaper changes.
She'll spoon-feed us hot cereal,
grown cold.

# My Dead Neighbors

He used to cook breakfast naked
(she used to tease him about that)
like in their first apartment,
where the elderly landlord
left his dead daughter's room untouched
because he still felt her suicide
nine years later (they never told me
if the girl left a note). Grease splashed him
more than once, and they'd embrace.
The bacon burned on those mornings,
but it was cold long before they were.

# Sounds of Loneliness

His fork scratches the plate
beneath scrambled eggs,
opposite chair empty.
Carelessly poured ketchup used to
make her nag him so much,
but now no one notices.
The waitress' accent
reminds him of the first time he paid for sex
a week ago-
thirty-some seconds failed to silence
twelve years still screaming goodbye.

Phone vibrates, ring tone impossible
to decide because he thinks everyone
he knows is so judgmental.
Wrong number, who sounds drunk,
calls back three more times.
His ex pocket dialed him yesterday,
stayed on the line for over twenty minutes-
he listened to all of it.

## overdue goodbye

darkness watches
a light left on
out of habit

windows frosted
door closed
only the wind knocks

snow silent as loneliness

# What Winter Sounds Like Now

Reminded of snowflakes melted on our tongues,
darkening sky could be your memory.
The storm begins as silent tears
hiding beneath a blanket too heavy for one;
wind quieter than arguments
long ended.
Eventual whiteout a lonely climax, missing
your joke about the polar bear in a blizzard.

## Last Season

Snowing again,
steps covered,
grass a memory
along with bare feet
on summer days
with no worries of slips,
broken hips,
doctor notes
justifying our frailties.

Safe on the wrong side
of a window, shut
tight, sky gone dull
like eyes that seen enough
and can't close,
but there will always be flowers
in the future,
sunlight reminding us
of nearing night.

# Because the Doctor Recommended Walking

Noticed a truck parked at your apartment,
and wonder if you're seeing someone new.

Why do my legs betray me nightly,
conspire with restless hands,
who miss the fingerprints they left to you?

Neither of us believes in heaven,
so how is this hell so real?

Blowing snow might as well be ash
falling from the devil's beard,
his laughter the cold wind
I can't escape.

## In Bed with a Fever

Evening breeze sneaks in,
cool against goosebumps,
even under blankets meant for two.

Beads of sweat are lies told
by a bored forehead,
who misses your nightly kiss.

Beneath dry tongue, sad words
scrape open cankers;
mouth stinks of pennies.

Pills help my temperature
countdown until darkness
can claim what's left of me.

Sleep brings a memory from summer:
you bra-less, soaked like a flower in rain,
your hand buried in my pants,

heat embraced until our bodies
beg us to stop—
we were never good listeners.

# Another Day

The first few minutes are the best
for forgetting the fight until she wakes up,
goes to the bathroom, and toilet flush
reminds him he pissed his pants.

He's hungover again; eyes feel empty,
brain stutters commands, tongue
tries to obey, but is too comfortable
lazing in their uncomfortable silence.

Coffee helps, makes her put clothes back on,
while their unmade bed stays quiet
as a dejected lover, who wore lingerie
when all he wanted was another six-pack.

# Growth

I miss the nothing days of my youth
when worry was a seed,
two stomachs rubbed
together like mittens,
white with the year's first snow.
Tears hid amongst rain in June,
puddles deeper than before.
Our unsaid words still colorful leaves,
your silence not yet a barren tree.
I miss the nothing days of our youth.

# It Doesn't Take Much to Break Us

We might as well be made from glass:
melted specs of sand,
shaped into something useful,
only to be shattered,
sometimes accidentally,
other times intentionally.

I wish we were joined by something
stronger.

# Third Date

I hate when the middle is still frozen,
what was supposed to be hot
cold on a fork washed by by hand,
and I chew and swallow because
it would be impolite to complain
after she cooked all afternoon,
after I kissed her cheek
when she moved towards my mouth.

# We Were always a Mirage

Encouraged by my overheated brain,
and my love of how sand
felt against my naked feet,
but you were always one drink away
from thin air,
so I packed an umbrella.

Another detail in our illusion:
Father Brown said you were cured,
gave us a bible; it sat
on our coffee table
like an empty bottle.

While you slowly sank deeper,
I died of thirst.

# lamentation

she wishes someone would play
with the hair on her arms
write a poem about it
or at least pin to the fridge
a note
saying anything other than
the dark silence that wallpapers
their room
every night separate blankets
backsides winning a staring contest

# Dining Alone

Firmer than our bed last night,
the booth presses against my tired backside.
Light reflects off the menu,
distorts my cataracted vision,
so I pretend to know what I want.
At a nearby table, a family
solemnly bow their heads,
faces aglow, transfixed by their phones.
Eventually, my meal arrives-
bacon atop eggs like a listless lover.

# Together

Their loneliness mutual
as a married couple's
shared silence
that feels more familiar
with every conversation left unsaid;
nights used only for snoring
and childish dreams
of yelling about broken backyard rules
and playing house. Happily ever after
easy when part of a game.

# Needs

You say we should visit a nude beach,
I laugh and imagine light
engulfing every sag,
while wrinkles lose their paleness,
replaced by sunburn,
the kind that peels for days after-wards,
but revealing nothing new
except some things need to be covered up.

# The Night Is Never Long Enough

Stars already invisible
from city lights,
midnight passes uncelebrated
except for a sleeping burp,
while blankets go unshared
again,
but then morning lingers,
bed left unmade,
coffee aroma fixes
morning breath that stinks
of reheated soup and crackers-
frost atop grass like an old lover.

# The North Is No Place for Love

Pines are probably jealous
of that leafless birch
with nothing left to hide.
Beneath its broken shade,
old snow starts to melt.
I try to sound sophisticated,
say the sky is still
as drying paint, brush
in God's back pocket;
you seem to ponder this
until grabbing me by my mitten,
and under that leafless birch-
toes a little less numb,
eyes close on our first kiss.

# September Snow

A hood hides your face
like clouds cover stars
as an early winter prepares
to bury dead leaves.

North is not a place
for love poems.
Hearts freeze here,
even when insulated by layers
only you have the patience
to remove and neatly fold.
Lips crack, with or without
the pressure of kissing,
my mittened hands
still cold.

# Loneliness Is Rarely Imagined

I want to walk and count snowflakes
with you, only to stop:
hood peeled back, hat fallen,
palm naked on red cheek,
fingertips warm against cold neck-
our kiss
meticulous as old love poems
no one has the time to write anymore.
But instead, my footprints punctuate
another day's end, and yours
go in the opposite direction.

# Wrong

Alone and shirtless again,
whiskey my only friend with advice;
ice cubes cracked long after I was.

Each sip whispers, "Call her,
even if it's midnight, tell her
you'll make coffee in the morning,

joke how only her fingernails
can scratch your hairy back,
that you'll moan like a walrus,

yet beg her to look into your eyes
as you kiss, so she knows how serious
this all is- that she is worthy of poems."

But my fingers misremember her number,
and I talk to Debbie for half an hour,
she had hip surgery last Tuesday.

# About the Author

Richard LeDue was born in Sydney, Nova Scotia, Canada, but currently lives in Norway House, Manitoba, with his wife and son. His poems have appeared in various publications throughout 2019 and 2020, including his first chapbook from Kelsay Books.

www.ingramcontent.com/pod-product-compliance
Lightning Source LLC
Chambersburg PA
CBHW071642090426
42738CB00013B/3193